100 THINGS You Can Do TO KEEP YOUR FAMILY TOGETHER...

when it sometimes seems like the whole world is trying to pull it apart

MARGE KENNEDY

Peterson's
Princeton, New Jersey

Library of Congress Cataloging-in-Publication Data

Kennedy, Marge M., 1950-
    100 things you can do to keep your family together—when it sometimes seems like
    the whole world is trying to pull it apart/Marge Kennedy
    p.   cm.
    ISBN 1-56079-340-6
    1. Family—Miscellanea. I. Title. II. Title: One hundred things you can do to keep
    your family together.
306.85—dc20   94-21833
                                                                          CIP

◈◈ Contents

Introduction

PART ONE: DISCOVERING
YOUR FAMILY'S HISTORY AND HOPES

PART TWO: CELEBRATING
YOUR FAMILY'S SPECIAL DAYS AND WAYS

PART THREE: CONNECTING WITH YOUR COMMUNITY

PART FOUR: MAKING LEMONADE—TURNING STRESS POINTS TO YOUR ADVANTAGE

❧ Introduction

Out of my mother, Ruth's, and my father, William's, most traditional of marriages, came five children, each of whom has come to define family in somewhat different ways. Kathy, the oldest, recently celebrated her 27th wedding anniversary with her and her husband, Tony's, three grown children, Laura (who's about to marry Tom), Michael, and Scott. The next one, Kevin, grew up and married Karen, who had two children, Kim and Jim, from an earlier marriage. Their blended family grew with the birth of their son David. Kevin died in 1993 at the age of 47. Ann, the fourth child, married Anthony and they recently adopted a baby girl whom they've named Beth. John, the youngest, is so far single. I am a single mother of five-year-old Caitlin.

For me and my siblings, the family we grew up with gave us our perspective, and the families we've helped create give us that and more. It will be the same for our children. And for theirs.

Within each new branch are other family members—cousins, nieces, and nephews by marriage, best friends who are just as much a part of our extended families as those born, adopted, or married into it. Each generation, of course, has a different vantage point on this particular family. Indeed, within each generation, each person experiences his or her place in the constellation differently.

It's a wonderfully messy arrangement, in which relationships overlap, underlie, support, and oppose one another. It didn't always come together easily nor does it always stay together easily.   It's known very good times and very bad ones. It has held together, often out of shared memories and hopes, sometimes out of the lure of my sisters' cooking, and sometimes out of sheer stubbornness. And like the world itself, our family is renewed by each baby.

100 Things You Can Do To Keep Your Family Together...when it seems like the whole world is trying to pull it apart is also about renewal, the kind that comes from making connections to those around us, and from keeping those connections alive even when the people we love most are driving us crazy. I hope that this book provides your family with ideas for celebrating and renewing itself and that you have as much fun reading it as I had writing it. Enjoy!

This book is dedicated to the memory of my parents,
Ruth and William, and to the hopes of their grandchildren.

The author wishes to thank the many friends and relatives who offered suggestions for this book and her editor, Carol Hupping, for encouraging her all the way.

Part One ❖

DISCOVERING YOUR FAMILY'S HISTORY AND HOPES

It's an odd thing when you think about it, but you and your children are born with a history. It's much more than a biological lineage. Each of us enters the world because hope for the future preceded us. No matter how you and your children came to be part of your particular clan, you and they are carving out a piece of the world that is uniquely yours. Moreover, each of you sees this place from a particular vantage point. Finding and appreciating each separate strand enriches the whole.

1 ❧ Write a Letter to Your Children

What were your thoughts when you first held your child? Did he or she remind you of anyone? Why did you choose the name you did? In the rush of living, it's all too easy to forget the reasons behind all the bustle. But when quiet times do occur, take a moment to write a letter to each of your children. It will clarify for you now and for your children later just why your family matters so much.

I was a typical teenager, I guess. In any case, my mother and I couldn't seem to connect on anything. One day when I was 17, we were having a truly horrific fight and both of us said some awful things. Me especially. I hated her for not making more of her life. I was afraid, I guess, that I would be like her someday. Each of us had retreated to our own rooms, but she knocked on my door, came in, and handed me a pile of letters—18 of them—one from the day I was born and one that she'd written on each of my birthdays. I found out so much more about her, about me, too, than I'd never known. After that, things changed. Now I'm 37 and I realize that the best of me is indeed like my mother. And I'm glad of that.

—Charlotte

2 ❧ …And Now Let's Go to the Videotape

Modern times may challenge family togetherness, but modern machinery can capture and preserve essential information about your family's days and ways as no still photograph ever could. If you don't already own a video recorder, rent or borrow one and go off in search of relatives near and far to record their impressions of life.

GETTING YOUR STORY

❖ Ask specific questions to jog memories: *Where did she meet her spouse? How did he celebrate his 21st birthday? In what kind of crib did their first child sleep? What was her first day at work like?*

❖ For those who do not feel comfortable being interviewed, ask to be taken on a guided tour of his or her home, pointing out the history of various furnishings, utensils, even old clothes.

❖ Have an older relative who actually knows who all those people in your ancient photo album are "walk" you through the album, while you zoom in on the various photos and record your relative's verbal captions.

❖ Involve the kids—have them ask and answer questions, too.

❖ Create a musical score by playing appropriate background music.

3 ❧ Where Did I Come From?

As any parent knows, this question could mean one of two things when a kid is doing the asking. Let's assume for the moment that your son or daughter is not asking about the birds and the bees and instead is just a bit curious about your family's genealogy. (Whew!)

Every family traveled some path to get to where it is today. Use a world map to help your children locate countries, states, and cities near and far that were once (and may still be) home to family members. Tell what you know of the reasons for their travels. Celebrate an ethnic holiday together. Learn a few words of your ancestors' language(s). Write to tourist boards and historical societies to find out about various places that gave root to your family tree.

TOOLS TO HELP YOU
DISCOVER SOME FAMILY HISTORY

❖ U.S. Census Bureau records, categorized by state and going back to 1790, can be found in local libraries.

❖ Copies of birth, death, and marriage records as well as property deeds and wills can be obtained through county courthouses in the locale that each event took place. For baptismal, marriage, and burial records, also check church archives.

❖ For information on obtaining census, immigration, military, and government pension data, send a self-addressed stamped envelope (two stamps) to the National Archives and Records Administration, General Reference Branch, Washington, D.C. 20408.

❖ A brochure, "Suggestions for Beginners in Genealogy," is available by sending a two-stamp self-addressed envelope to the National Genealogical Society, 4527 17th Street North, Arlington, VA 22207-2399.

4 ◈ 2001 Time Capsule

The 21st-century is not so many years away. Celebrate yourselves as the living legends of *this* century by creating a family time capsule.

Nothing really fancy is required—just a container that will hold some of the artifacts that represent your family at this time. Seal the container with the promise to open it on New Year's Day 2001. Store it in a safe place, or, for added drama, bury your time capsule in a retrievable location.

CONSIDER INCLUDING

◈ photographs
◈ drawings
◈ diary entries
◈ a current issue of *TV Guide* (with each family member's favorite shows marked off)
◈ the program from a child's school event
◈ a container from a frequented fast-food place
◈ a telephone directory
◈ a piece of costume jewelry
◈ an item of clothing
◈ a wrapped surprise from each person

5 ✧ Post a Postcard Chain

With friends and families scattered around the globe, it can be hard to keep in touch with everyone and even harder to give the kids a sense of just where everybody is. Sending letters seems to take too much time; phone calls can be expensive and when they're over, you've got nothing tangible to hold onto.

The next time you're sending out holiday greeting cards, birth announcements, or any other "mass mailing," add a photocopied request that asks each recipient to mail a postcard of his or her hometown to you and other family members on a particular date—such as the first day of spring.

Make sending—and receiving—these cards with quick-to-write and easy-to-read notes an annual tradition.

An Invitation to Start a Tradition

What: An annual postcard exchange

Where: From your house to ours—and everyone else on this list

When: Every June 21

cc: Uncle Joe: 15 Main Street, Maplewood, TN 07726

Aunt Isabel: 4332 Birch Lane, Ellington, VT 60008

Cousin Tina: 3 rue de Maissoneuve, Paris, France

6 ❧ Create a Family Flag

Countries, states, and clubs do it. Surely your family is every bit as much a distinctive entity as an organized political or social group. With a little thought and discussion, you and your family can identify appropriate symbols, colors, and other elements that make your statement. For instance, a family of sports enthusiasts can borrow the Olympic five-ring design, substituting those five colors (which represent colors from each member nation's flag) for family favorites. Look for plays on your name to create your symbols: the Greenbaum family may choose a fir tree symbol; the Bakers, a pie; and the Gills, a school of fish, for example. Incorporate your family's crest or coat of arms or the flag from your family's country of origin.

For material, use a cloth pillowcase, felt, or paper. Apply your design with ink or paint, or for the more ambitious, with needlework.

SEVEN FLAG FLYING OPPORTUNITIES

1. Family reunions
2. Birthdays
3. Family picnics
4. Holidays
5. Anniversaries
6. Birth of a new family member
7. Greeting visiting relatives

7 ◈ Pass Down a Family Heirloom

The first time I came across my grandmother's graduation ring, I was about seven. I begged my mother to let me wear it. This went on for years until the ring finally moved from my mother's dresser drawer to my right hand when I was 16. She swore I'd lose it. I swore I wouldn't.

During my years of wearing it, I have felt an incredible connectedness to my grandmother that surprises me.

Someday I hope to give it to my daughter. At age five, she's already expressed interest in it. I told her she'd just lose it. She swears she wouldn't. We've agreed she can have it when she's 16.

I had it appraised once. It's worth about 20 dollars. And much, much more.

NOT-SO-OBVIOUS HEIRLOOMS

- tools
- cookbooks
- rites of passage mementos such as First Communion veils, Bar Mitzvah yarmulkes, graduation caps, birthday cake decorations
- documents such as a first driver's license, marriage certificates, etc.
- newspapers and magazines from a person's date of birth

8 ❖ "Star Light, Star Bright"

Whether you live in the country under a blanket of stars or in the city, where finding a star above the city lights takes a bit more attention, noting that first star and sing-songing the child's nursery rhyme can be a special part of many an evening. Verbalizing your wishes aloud and together brings a lovely wind-down moment to your family's day and can give you all insight into each other's hopes and dreams.

ADDITIONAL WISHING OPPORTUNITIES

❖ Wishing wells—including public fountains, lakes, and even puddles. At a penny a wish, it's quite a bargain.
❖ Candles on cakes for no special occasion at all—just the fun of blowing them out.
❖ Anything that you and your family do once in a while. For instance: Make a wish whenever you double-knot a shoelace, rinse shampoo out of hair, cross paths with a cat, or find a coin.

9 ⚙ When I Was Your Age...

Until they're about age seven, kids willingly and enthusiastically buy into the idea that their parents are perfect. While you wouldn't want to blow the myth totally or prematurely, it can be freeing for all of you to set the record straight and share some of your own growing-up foibles.

Stories that invite our kids in to our own pasts give them insight into problem solving, allow them to forgive themselves for their perceived inadequacies, and serve as good person-to-person (and not just parent-to-child) touchpoints—something we all need as kids come to understand the limits of our perfection.

Let them know about the time in kindergarten when you didn't quite make it to the little girls' room, about the time you beheaded all of your sister's dolls, or the time you dropped your grandmother's turkey dinner platter on the floor just before Thanksgiving dinner was to be served. Choose stories that don't make you the hero and that don't necessarily have happy, moralistic endings, but rather that simply give kids a picture of you as a normal, regular kid.

10 ◈ Share Superstitions

W hat falls on the floor comes in the door." With this particular Irish superstition, intoned mostly at mealtimes, a fork represents a woman, a spoon means a child, and a knife heralds a soon-to-arrive male visitor. Every culture, including the subculture of each individual family, has in its recent or distant past a set of superstitious beliefs that defy logic in their primitive evocation of good and evil spirits. Few of us have been immune to the power of superstitious thinking, nor need we be when we consider how much fun can be had by approaching these beliefs playfully. Remember sing-songing, "Step on a crack and break your mother's back"? It turned a simple walk home into a superheroic quest to protect Mom.

Where can you go to find superstitions worth passing along? Start with your family's older relatives. Without disparaging others' beliefs, relate to your kids stories such as how "Grandma always said that finding a penny heads up was good luck and finding one tails up meant bad news was coming." Look at the superstition-based rituals you enjoy and try to figure out if any of them indeed signaled what was to come: Was the bridesmaid who caught the bouquet the next woman to marry? Ask librarians and booksellers to recommend books on cultural superstitions. Invent one or two of your own.

In these modern times, we can miss the satisfaction that comes from turning to the otherworldly to enrich everyday events or to explain mundane occurrences.

11 ❖ Quilt-Making for Modern Times

When fabric was scarce and nothing was wasted, old clothes were not discarded but were turned into useful and artful quilts. Few of us today have the time, energy, or expertise for elaborate quilting, and used clothing, of which we have so much, is often passed along in nearly new condition. So what can we do with the few scraps of material we have collected that are not appropriate for giving away, and the lack of time and talent that can keep us from recycling both cloth and memories?

❖ Collect fabric from children's clothing that is beyond the passing-down stage. Fortunately the most worn-out pieces are also likely to be among their favorites. There's no need to have enough material for a complete quilt when you start. *Then:*

❖ Buy a quilt with applique designs already on it. As material becomes available, trace the applique design onto paper and use it as a pattern. Cut out a new overlay to sew over that portion of the ready-made quilt. *Or:*

❖ Instead of making a quilt, cut a three-inch star or other shape from a variety of old fabrics. Later on, decorate denim jackets or other clothing with them. For instance, sew on the stars from childhood clothing to present to your 13-year-old on her birthday, or to your 18-year-old as he heads off for college.

12 ❦ Create a Portrait Gallery

Those wonderful, formal tintypes from generations passed mixed with portraits and snapshots of your family in more recent times will allow everyone to see where you've been and where you're going. To enhance the already honorable display, consider these ideas:

❖ Use indirect lighting to preserve the quality of the photos.

❖ Rather than having all portraits hung on the walls, place some on small tables and some on shelves.

❖ Put photos in frames that are reminiscent of the period.

❖ Have photos taken of your generation dressed and posed in the same manner as the oldest photos.

❖ If possible, include your own childhood photos alongside your children's photos. (So often and so easily, our kids forget that we ourselves were ever that young.)

❖ Label all pictures identifying the people, the occasion, and the place where the photo was taken.

❖ Intersperse other memorabilia, such as religious icons, framed documents, blue ribbons and certificates, children's artwork, etc.

❖ Give copies of your favorites to relatives to share the pleasure and to ensure that irreplaceable photos are preserved.

13 ⊗ Enter Contests and Sweepstakes

They arrive in the mailbox by the caseload, those sweepstakes entries that proclaim, "You may already be a millionaire!" Putting cynicism aside for a moment, it can be fun to imagine together just what you and your family would do with a million bucks. Sometimes, talking about such a fortune can give you insight into each other's hopes and dreams.

"I'd take ballet lessons!" said one seven-year-old, surprising her mother who didn't even know the child was interested in taking dance classes. Another friend reports that when his son said, "I'd pay off all your bills," he realized just how much out-loud worrying he'd been doing; the conversation gave him a chance to reassure his kid that his complaints about money didn't mean that the family was broke.

For any family, imagining a month on a tropical island, season tickets to a favorite sports event, or a chance to live in a palace can be just plain fun. Talking about scads of money and what it could mean also gives parents the opportunity to remind themselves and their kids just how rich in each other's company they already are.

14 ❖ Read All About It

What was the big news item on the day *you* were born? Besides the birth of *your* first child, what else happened on that memorable day? A visit to your local library will help you uncover original newspapers and magazines that bear the date of birth of each family member. Make two photocopies of each pertinent front page, then give one to each person and keep the other in a safe place for passing down to your grandchildren.

EXTRA! EXTRA!

To add to your historic record, you can also research to find out:

❖ Names of the president, governor, and mayor at the time of each person's birth
❖ The best-selling book and top record album
❖ Some hot fads
❖ The political hot spots
❖ The most popular TV show (for those born after 1950 only!) or the top radio program
❖ Something about current fashion
❖ An invention that made its debut that year

15 ✹ They're Playing Our Song

Songs, like certain scents, evoke strong memories. The tune played at your wedding, the lullaby your baby enjoyed most, the song that your child first learned to sing, the hymn played at your grandparent's funeral.

Songs are like markers, and hearing one that meant something special brings forth a flood of sensations that mere words do not.

Ask each member of your family to tell you which songs matter the most to him or her and why. Try recording these onto a single tape, "The _____ Family's Greatest Hits."

16 ❖ The Mail-Order Reunion

Nothing really beats getting together in person, but not getting together need not be the same as losing touch.

Involve your kids and all the cousins in an effort to create a mail-order reunion. Ask someone from each branch of the family tree to collect written recollections of important events, recipes, photocopies of black and white photos, and other reproducible memorabilia.

Offer to act as editor by collecting and assembling the materials and resending a complete staple-bound copy to each family. Suggest that each year a different teen be responsible for gathering new material.

17 ❧ Special Delivery Boxes

The first pair of shoes, kindergarten artwork, report cards, a lock of hair. These are the remains of childhood. Often they're saved in bottom dresser drawers and other corners of our lives, too precious to be thrown out but too scattered to be cherished.

For each child, prepare a special box into which you place a few mementos of each growing-up year, to be given to that child on another momentous occasion, such as a school graduation or the birth of his or her first child.

When I got married, my mother, a real pack-rat, gave me a cardboard box covered in the wallpaper of the room my sister and I used to share. At first I thought it was just more of mom's junk, and I kidded her about finally being able to unload some of her stuff onto me. When I finally got around to looking at it, I found things like the Mother's Day cards I'd made her, my Communion prayer book, even my first tooth. Now I have two kids of my own, and while I'm not the saver my mother was, I am keeping a box for each of them. What's just as much fun as saving their stuff is going through my box with them. And one time, it really saved me. My son lost his first lost tooth and was afraid that the Tooth Fairy wouldn't visit. I pretended that I'd found it—actually my own long-lost tooth—and placed it under his pillow.

—Nancy

18 ❖ Tell Tales

There are few who can resist listening raptly to true stories told with gusto—especially when the star of the tale is the one doing the listening. Kids never tire of hearing the story of the day they became part of the family, of their accomplishments, and even of their foibles if they're encouraged to laugh along instead of feeling laughed at. Everyone needs reminders that the fact of their being on this earth is important and that each life changes everything.

My parents, as long as I could remember, told and retold the story of the day they first decided to adopt me and the day they finally took me home. I was about two when they adopted me and always that story—about me tossing my socks at them from my crib, about the snowstorm that left them stranded on the highway for the whole night on their way back home, about the red dress my mom had made me—felt like the greatest adventure tale of all time.

I don't know if I actually remember all the incidents but it feels like I do. I heard the stories so many times as I was growing up that the memory was always right there, really alive.

—Christina

19 ◈ This Is Your Life

Back in the late 1950s, one night a week most of the 50 million TV sets in the U.S. were tuned in to "This Is Your Life." For half an hour, participants and viewers alike, recalled the people and places that stood out as landmarks in one person's life. Updated and now focusing on celebrities instead of ordinary folk, it's back on the air. Maybe it's time to make an episode all your own.

Some occasions naturally conjure up a review of the past—birthdays, anniversaries, reunions. And while these events are just right for recollections, it isn't really necessary to hook a retrospective on any particular event. Imagine a loved one's reaction if you were to gather people and mementos for an all-out review of the characters and events that helped make him or her the terrific person you're now celebrating.

PLANNING YOUR SHOW

◈ Start planning about three months ahead of time.

◈ Arrange photos—going back to infancy, if possible, and continuing to the present—in a special album.

◈ Prepare a form letter/invitation to send out to old friends, classmates, former teachers, etc., explaining the upcoming celebration and asking them to write a letter with a recollection of the "star" for your album.

◈ Call his or her former schools for copies of records and archive photos.

◈ Check attics and garages for additional mementos.

◈ On your last filled-in page, pen a letter about why you're glad that he or she is part of your life.

◈ Leave 20 or so pages blank so the recipient can continue to add his or her own thoughts and souvenirs of life.

20 ❖ Explore the Spiritual Together

Parents, whether or not we believe in a deity, know that to witness a child's mind searching for meaning is a miracle. Accompanying a child on that search, sometimes guiding her, sometimes holding back and letting her look in places we might never have approached, enriches everyone's understanding of the world and each other.

Some families find that belonging to a community of like-thinkers (or fellow explorers) gives them the framework with which to respond to their children's need for answers on spiritual matters.

Others find that simply living their lives according to a moral and thoughtful code of conduct gives kids the parameters they need to explore their spiritual selves.

The important thing, most would agree, is giving our kids the safety of knowing that questioning is part of the human condition and that their search for answers will be met with respect.

21 ⊗ Share Dreams

My five-year-old, as usual, was balking at waking up. "I was having a good dream, and you interrupted it!" she howled. Her anger grew when she realized that, in the instant that her feet hit the floor, she'd forgotten what the dream was about. "Mom," she pleaded, "tell me what happened." I said, "How could I possibly know what happened? It was your dream." She answered, "You can to remember it. You were *in* it!"

The dreams of sleep have that wonderful and sometimes bizarre way of feeling so real that it's hard to accept their intangible nature. Leaving analysis of dreams aside, it's fun to recount to one another your nocturnal adventures. After all, where else but in a dream can you star in your own sci-fi movie, run for President, or attend a party with the likes of Julius Caesar?

Sharing our dreams with those who matter most in our waking hours can be a great way to deepen our understanding of each other and ourselves. Keep a dream notebook by your bedside and encourage kids to do the same. Make a rule that no one reads one another's entries, but agree to make an effort to unveil a few dreams now and again—especially those that cast other family members in particularly inspiring roles.

22 ❧ Cook Up a Family Cookbook

Gathering around the hearth, relying on Great-grandma's recipes to turn your home-grown bounty into a sumptuous feast—this is the stuff of nostalgia that made Norman Rockwell famous. It's more than likely that we don't hunt and gather all our own food; it's possible that we get most of our recipes from the backs of macaroni boxes; it's even true that we can't always sit down together for evening meals. But these realities don't negate the centrality of food in our lives. Food provides more than physical sustenance; eating together is emotionally filling, too.

You don't have to be a good cook to include a few favorite meals in your weekly menu of activity. And writing down each family member's favorite dish and how to prepare it—even if it is just plain spaghetti or tuna salad—gives you a neat record of who likes what.

Expand your cookbook by adding clippings from magazines and newspapers of things you'd like to try. Ask friends and relatives to donate a few ideas. When your child comes home bragging about Mr. Ludlum's homemade pizza, ask for the recipe. You'll not only broaden your kitchen repertoire, you'll be creating a document that will allow growing-up kids to learn just how to make the meals that matter most to them.

23 ◈ Create a New Holiday Tradition

Boy meets girl. Boy marries girl. Boy and girl angst over which family they visit at Thanksgiving and which one in December and whether or not it's best to serve turkey or goose for the family feast.

When first faced with the reality that the family you married into does things differently, the warmth of tradition can take on a chill. Each tradition feels right to the one bringing it to the table. Many families try to compromise, but that can leave everyone feeling that something essential is missing. Another approach is for parents and kids to find out together what each person's favorite tradition really is, why it matters to him or her, and to see if it or something entirely new would best satisfy the emotional need that traditions and rituals are made to fill.

John's family always had a big dinner and then opened their Christmas presents on Christmas Eve, which, to me, spoiled the anticipation of Christmas morning. In my family, Christmas Eve was for Midnight Mass and caroling. Until the kids were about four and five, we took turns—one year doing it "his" way and one year doing it "mine." Then, about three years ago, we were asked to help out at the church's soup kitchen on Christmas Eve. We took the kids along and we all pitched in. It was the best Christmas Eve we ever had as a family. And now that's our tradition. I suppose when each of our kids gets married, she'll think that this is what you're supposed to do, too.

—Linda

24 ❧ Learn the History of the Site of Your Home

Fifty years ago, it might have been a stretch of farmland. One hundred years ago, a forest. A hundred years before that, it could have been a native tribe's hunting ground. Prehistorically? It's not as impossible as you might think to find out who (or what) may have walked the soil beneath your foundation and what history might be buried beneath the stone.

To find out more recent history, check building and tax records in your town. If the house and neighborhood predate you, talk to older neighbors and ask them to share their memories with you.

To find out what transpired before buildings claimed the space, check with your local historical society, the history departments of local colleges, and the library. Read old newspapers and documents. Old maps and photographs, particularly, bring the past home as you compare today's highways and highrises to another era's lay of the land.

25 ✿ Revisit the Old Homestead

Even if the old family place was a walk-up apartment on the outskirts of St. Louis, an expedition to the place where your family planted its modern roots can bear fruit for you and your kids. Don't be afraid of what sadness it might bring. After all, nothing is the same as it once was, and that's not an altogether bad thing.

Before you go, check the current telephone book to see if there might be someone you knew from back then who's still there and with whom you can visit. If the old neighborhood has given way to the on-ramp to Route 70, take the trip anyway and look for other, still-remaining landmarks. Let your kids see the school you or their grandparents attended, the hospital where you were born, the farmland you once ran across, places where great-grandparents are buried.

Seeing where you came from not only gives children a better understanding of you as a person, it better prepares them for accepting and celebrating the ever-changing landscape of their own lives.

Part Two ❧

CELEBRATING YOUR FAMILY'S SPECIAL DAYS AND WAYS

Birthdays, anniversaries, rites-of-passage events like weddings and graduations—these are the hooks upon which we hang the years. By celebrating important events, we are, of course, celebrating each other. But it's the everyday stuff—off-to-school mornings, suppers, Saturday mornings—that really give substance to our lives and provide us with the opportunity to enjoy and embrace the mundane, making every day special in its own way.

26 ✧ What's in a Name?

In an effort to make picking up a deck of animal-picture cards a bit more fun," a mother of a preschooler recalls, "I asked my daughter to help me name all the animals as we picked up each card from the floor. She readily agreed to join in. I picked up the first card and was about to say 'elephant,' when she called out 'Peter.' Then picking up the duck card, she shouted, 'Jack.' Her baby cousin Peter's favorite toy was his stuffed elephant. And 'Jack,' of course, was from her favorite book, *Make Way for Ducklings.*" Clearly, this child understood that names are full of meaning for everyone, not merely labels that help differentiate one from the other.

As parents, we sometimes choose names simply for the lovely sounds they make. Sometimes, a child's name honors another family member. Occasionally, we choose a name to instill a sense of ethnic or historical connectedness to our offspring. Whatever reason you had for choosing your child's name, let your child know. Buy or rent a book about names to look up the meaning of each family member's name. Consider together ways in which each name is just right for each child.

27 ❖ The Name Game, Part 2

What's really in a name? Letters, of course! And with a little imagination, anyone's name can be dissected and reconstructed to describe each moniker's true meaning. You can help kids learn some great new vocabulary words while you're at it. Here are some examples to get you started.

Using descriptive adjectives:
T - errific
A - rtistic
R - ambunctious
A - miable

Using hobbies and other activities:
T - umbling
A - erobics
R - unning
A - cting

MORE NAME GAMES:

❖ Tell kids how you arrived at your nicknames for them.
❖ Share some of the nicknames you had as a kid.
❖ Ask kids what names they might have chosen for themselves if they'd had a say in the matter.
❖ Look in encyclopedias and volumes of *Who's Who* to find other important people who share your and your children's names.
❖ Help everyone learn his or her name in another language.

28 ◈◈ Make Handprints

When you have kids in the house, handprints covering walls and everything else are necessarily part of the decor. Making additional handprints on purpose may put some parents over the edge, but it actually can be fun and add a distinctive decorating element to your home. Consider the possibilities:

◈ Put the finishing touches on a newly painted child's room by adding a colorful border design around doors, window frames, or elsewhere by having each child who shares the room (or a single occupant) press his/her hand into a shallow plate of complementary-colored paint and pressing it carefully onto the wall, repeating the process until the desired area is covered.

◈ Apply handprints to mirrors or furnishings, which can turn a garage-sale item into a one-of-a-kind designer piece and a future heirloom.

◈ For gift-giving to doting grandparents and for saving for yourself, make plaster-of-Paris casts of children's handprints in pie tins.

◈ Make an everyday (as opposed to holiday) wreath by tracing every family member's handprint onto heavy cardboard (multiple copies of handprints may be needed) and stapling them together in a circular pattern. Add some special touches, like costume-jewelry bracelets, watches, and rings, and maybe some cuffs from outgrown shirts and blouses.

29 ✧ He Said/She Said: The _____ Family Book of Quotations

They represent a child's innocence, her confusion about language ("Mom, how come Grandma always calls me a deer?"), or his frustration at being a kid (as one five-year-old told his dad—who had just noted that he couldn't read without his glasses—"Please buy me some glasses so I can read, too.").

They can make us laugh or cry or sometimes both. They are the ridiculous and endearing statements our kids make that we swear we'll never forget.

But we do forget. Start a book to jot down your kids' sure-to-be famous quotations. Any notebook will do. Keep it in an easy-to-get place and at least once a week, reach for it and update it with the best sayings you've overheard.

30 ◇◇ Create Self-Portraits

When was the last time you drew a picture of yourself? Chances are good that it was back in kindergarten. By the time most of us are preteens, we are deceived into thinking that results are more important than the process. Young kids whose inhibitions haven't taken hold know better and will happily spend hours reinventing themselves on paper.

The results, in fact, are always beautiful. With your kids, why not try making self-portraits again? One exercise that can help you recall the delightfully slow-paced and self-loving motions that go into rendering oneself on paper is to begin by sketching portraits of your kids.

Neat, huh? Now each of you can spend some time around the dining-room table drawing yourselves—and each other. Proudly display the work for all to see.

31 ❖ Get Away from It All

Routine provides us with the structure we need to get from here to there every day. Without set times for meeting set responsibilities, our days would be even more chaotic than they already are. But with the safety of predictability in our lives comes a level of dreariness. How can we alter the cycle without spending a fortune on a two-week cruise or giving in completely to chaos? Here are five ideas for renewal:

1. Adjust the routine in fun ways. Instead of having dinner around the kitchen table, opt occasionally for a picnic—even one on the living room floor. Take a different route to work or home from school. Serve dessert first.

2. Ignore the mess. Once in a while, chuck your responsibilities and just enjoy one another. One mom tells of nearly despairing over the condition of her toy-strewn living room until, for one afternoon, she created a tent city out of sheets. Inside this relatively clutter-free space, she and her three-year-old twins told stories, ate lunch, and simply had fun without her being distracted by the many things she felt she "should" be doing.

3. Switch roles. Let the kids create dinner or prepare the shopping list while you watch TV.

4. Get away. Even if just for a single day, step into another world. City dwellers can head for the country; suburbanites to a city museum or cultural performance.

5. Pretend. Study up on a place you'd like to go but can't right now. Help the kids find it on a map, make a native dish, and rent some videos about it. Bon voyage.

32 ❖ Write Chain Letters

This variation on Idea 5 asks for notes written on 2" x 10" strips of paper instead of postcards. Here's how it works:

On a particular holiday, one on which decorations are displayed (such as Christmas or someone's birthday), have family members near and far write a wish or a message for each family on a strip of paper included with their greeting card.

Loop all of the messages together to form a chain, which then doubles as a celebration decoration that can be hung on the Christmas tree or looped above a door, window, or mirror.

33 ◈◈ Ten Things to Let Your Children Overhear You Say

Complimenting our kids directly can make them feel good. Letting them overhear us brag a bit about them when their backs are turned makes them feel great. Some well-earned phrases kids love to eavesdrop in on:

1. I'm proud of her.
2. He's a really terrific kid.
3. I can't right now; I'm having fun with my kids.
4. I'll ask my daughter; she's good at these things.
5. She did a great job!
6. We had so much fun together.
7. I'm not bragging, but....
8. The gift he made me was so perfect.
9. I love to watch her growing up.
10. I feel so lucky to be his parent.

34 ◈◈ Make Soup Together

Soup is a lot like a family. Each ingredient enhances the others; each batch has its own characteristics; and it needs time to simmer to reach full flavor. Even if the metaphor is stretching the bounds of good taste, making soup together is a perfect way to spend a cold evening.

Soup can be anything you want it to be and offers an opportunity for lots of experimentation. Any vegetables with any noodles and/or beans and/or rice with any broth will do.

Making soup without any particular recipe is a fun way to try out new ideas while clearing out the freezer and the cupboard. If your kids get to add a few ingredients of their own choosing, they're more likely to pronounce the results "delicious!" And now that you've got two quarts of it, you'll be glad you all made something that's sure to be eaten.

35 ❖ I've Been Framed

Kid Picassos create more works of art than most museums could handle. Saving it all is not really possible. Tossing it all would be a shame. To honor the efforts as well as the best results, try choosing one work each year from each kid to frame and display proudly.

One mom reports within earshot of her kindergartner: "It's the most amazing thing. But every year, Santa somehow finds my daughter's best work, frames it, and leaves it under the tree for me. And every year, it's my favorite gift."

TO SAVE AND TO SAVOR

Sometimes, a kid's best work is not a one-dimensional drawing. You can capture and conserve other accomplishments, too:

❖ Photograph a terrific block tower before getting to the necessary task of dismantling it to reclaim the living room floor.
❖ Tape record piano recitals, new songs learned, poetry readings.
❖ Create collages of special events—hair ribbons, a pressed flower, photo, program from a child's ballet recital, or ticket stubs from the season's final peewee soccer match.

36 ◈◈ Lights, Camera, Action!

Steven Spielberg learned his craft creating home movies. Surely there's a budding director under your roof, too. There are a number of "scripts" you can follow to capture the essence of your family on tape. For instance:

◈ *A Day in the Life*—Simply record the wonderfully mundane daily activities of your family, while you narrate.
◈ *Amateur Hour*—Who sings? Who dances? Who does magic tricks or recites poetry? Get it on tape.
◈ *Me Tarzan, You Jane*—Is there a favorite family movie you can reenact?
◈ *Candid Camera*—Remembering that this is a celebration of the life within your family, avoid recording potentially embarrassing or intrusive moments. Try instead to tape when people are already having a good time—such as at birthday parties—and work at capturing these events.

37 ✧ A Day in the Life, Part 2 (with single-use cameras)

Long before camcorders were invented, still photos captured the special moments of most American families. It's still a relatively new phenomenon to use the humble still-photo camera to record the everyday goings on. Again, it's modern technology that allows us to save the day—even the ordinary day.

Inexpensive, nearly indestructible single-use cameras are perfect for passing out to the kids without fear of them damaging our expensive and more delicate 35 millimeters. Letting kids loose with their own cameras gives them—and you—a chance to see things from their own very special perspective.

One wonderful activity is to create an album—"The Jones Family on March 10, 199_"—and to have each family member record whatever he or she wants for inclusion into this historic record.

38 ◈◈ Enjoy a Night on the Town

The informality of family life is a blessed condition that allows us all to become our best while looking our worst. Where else but in the comfort and familiarity of home can we wear our favorite torn bathrobe, lie on the sofa in the most undignified of positions, and allow our elbows to prop us up at the dinner table as we occasionally slurp our soup?

But every once in a while, it would be nice to show off our company clothes and manners just for one another. Try a no-special-occasion night out, with everyone wearing his or her finest. Skip the fast-food place and head for a restaurant with linens on the table and a multitude of silverware. Let the kids know that you're confident they'll strut their best stuff, and don't be afraid to bribe them for their good behavior with a promise of Death-by-Chocolate Cake for dessert.

And as one friend who tried this said, "I was able to relax and enjoy myself when I realized that it really didn't matter if the kids didn't behave perfectly. We all looked so good that nobody would have recognized us anyway!"

39 ◈◈ Say Thanks

It's undeniable: Even middle-aged middle managers feel a certain rush of satisfaction when a boss thanks them for a job well done. Let's face it, an acknowledgment of our contribution, even one that was just fulfilling an obligation, can make our day.

The same is true for our kids. Yes, they're expected to do their homework, maybe make their beds, and occasionally babysit for a younger brother or sister. All these things are part of being a family and doing one's part to keep it running. But wouldn't it be nice once every so often for a kid to hear, "Thanks for your help" or even "Thanks for being my kid."

There's no need to go overboard with praise (kids don't want to collect unearned accolades, anyway). But sincere thanks, especially coming from you, can more than make their day.

40 ❧ Help Your Kids Celebrate YOU!

We take great pleasure in planning our kids' birthday parties, congratulating them on a terrific report card, or for playing a winning soccer game. Rightly so, we don't expect our kids to show gratitude for taking care of them. That doesn't mean that they can't be helped to acknowledge us on days other than Mother's Day and Father's Day. Unlike spouses and good friends, however, kids need help in seeing us in any role besides being their parents. Let them in on the things that other people see and celebrate in you:

◆ Just got a job promotion? Buy yourself a gift on the way home and announce at the door that instead of the usual dinner, you're all going out for a night on the town. Be sure that the kids understand that you've just accomplished something terrific and that this celebration is for you.

◆ Did you do something that you really enjoyed? On those occasions when you caught a great movie, read a terrific book, heard a good joke, or anything else that gave you a moment's pleasure—and that had nothing at all to do with your being a parent—tell the kids about it. It will give them a bit of insight into you as a person.

◆ Birthday on the horizon? Give the kids plenty of notice that your big day is coming up, along with a few opportunities to earn some extra cash to buy you something nice. It never hurts to give them a few hints about what to buy you, either.

41 ◈◈ Play Board Games

There are a few things about board games that make them perfect for family togeth-erness: They encourage you all to sit more or less face to face; they can be played one-on-one or in teams (allowing a very young player to play alongside an older, more experienced player); and you don't have to know a thing about electronics to play—a particular bonus to technophobic parents. To keep the games as fun as they're meant to be, remember:

◈ Kids under age five or so will have trouble playing by rules and even more trouble los-ing. Help a young player learn the rules one step at a time, playing practice games. Give them some experience on how to lose gracefully by intentionally taking turns winning and losing.

◈ To equalize the playing field a bit, give younger players a starting advantage. For instance, in checkers, the older, more experienced player can begin with fewer men on the board.

◈ Let all players take turns choosing the games.

◈ Help usually rivalrous siblings team up to play you, encouraging the older sister or brother to share winning strategies with the younger player.

◈ Have the winner put away the game board and playing pieces.

42 ◈◈ Let Your Kids Teach You Something You Don't Know

It can be exhausting to be the one who knows everything. "I saw a confidence in my son I never saw before one day when he was trying to explain to me what was going on in a football game," says one non-athletic mother, admitting that it was the first time either of them could recall where he'd definitely been the more knowledgeable of the two of them.

After years of demonstrating how to tie shoelaces, spell, and eat with a semblance of civility, it's easy to forget that kids are nevertheless out there gathering information that didn't come from us. Watch what happens when your son or daughter gets to teach you how to roller blade, program the VCR, or French braid your hair. You'll both find out what they're good at, you'll learn some new skill, and your kids will enjoy trying out the parental/teaching role.

43 &&& Go on an Amusement Park Ride Together

No doubt, the kids have heard you scream. Even the most self-controlled parent lets loose now and then with a tirade about missing sneakers or incomplete homework. Occasional familial outbursts don't necessarily do much harm, but they're not the things that fond memories are made of either.

Sharing some screams as you and your kids zoom down the sheer cliff of a roller coaster, however, can create sheer magic. You're in this thing together, hanging on for dear life, anticipating, experiencing, thrilling. It's a lot like your lives together, just at a higher pitch.

If high speed tumbles are not your style, join your kids for a visit to the haunted mansion, a jaunt on the bumper cars, or a nice, sedate turn around on the carousel. You'll all enjoy the moment.

44 ❧ Take Lessons Together

Kids and parents rarely start any activity with the same level of competence. The usual pattern is for parents to teach kids some new skill or to turn the kid over to a qualified teacher while we just sit outside the practice room and write a check.

Seeing you struggle to master something new alongside them gives many kids the impetus to strive a bit harder. It's fun to compete with Mom or Dad, especially when they've got a chance at coming out ahead.

Some added benefits of learning along with your kids include giving them a chance to see how you overcome frustration and work through any difficulties.

SOME IDEAS FOR TANDEM LEARNING

- car repair
- cooking
- snorkeling
- juggling
- computer graphics
- fishing
- cross-country skiing
- a foreign language

45 ❖ Have an Un-Birthday Party

Each family's personal calendar follows a predictable melody. There are the rhythms of the school year overlaid by the rhythms of the holidays you celebrate and punctuated by your and your children's anniversaries and birthdays, creating lulls and crescendoes that are uniquely yours.

You can enrich this musical score by splicing in some new holidays of your own making. Kids particularly, who eagerly announce each fraction of their ages ("Are you five?" "No! I'm five and a half!"), will appreciate a formal acknowledgment of their new status. A family-only un-Birthday party says you noticed. Another option for an un-Birthday party is simply to pick a time of year when nothing much else is going on and declare it your entire family's un-Birthday party.

AN UN-BIRTHDAY PARTY SAMPLER

If you're celebrating a child's half-year:

❖ Celebrate a half-birthday with half a cake.
❖ Put the correct number of candles in—six and a half for a child that age.
❖ Play Pin-the-Tail on the Donkey with only the relevant half of the donkey displayed.
❖ Let the celebrating child watch an extra half-hour of TV or stay up and extra half-hour later.

If you're celebrating everyone's un-birthday:

❖ Choose names and make a gift for the person whose name you've chosen.
❖ Buy something special that the whole family can enjoy—a bushel basket of flavored popcorn, personalized bath towels, a professionally taken family photo.

46 ❖ Redecorate

While a full-scale renovation may be on your long-term list of things to do, there are usually a host of interim home-improvement projects that will make you and your family all feel better about your environment right now. None have to cost much in either money or time. To make redecorating less of a chore and more of a family activity:

❖ Decide together what project could benefit everyone—new bookshelves, a homework center, a sports-equipment storage closet.
❖ Divvy up the work according to family members' abilities; even a four-year-old can assist in painting or toy organizing; a ten-year-old is old enough to learn how to use some power tools with your direct supervision.
❖ Take everyone's tastes into consideration; for instance, there may be a way to work in some deep purple trim into your project, thus satisfying your preteen's need to make a statement.

47 ◈ Create a Family Bulletin Board

At first it may appear to be yet another attempt at trying to organize your family, but a family bulletin board can be a celebration of family life, too. It's the place to keep the family calendar, maybe one that's color coded (a separate color for each person's entry or red for "must do's" and green for the "fun stuff"). Here's where you can post messages and reminders to one another, including simple, unexpected love notes. It's where you can display achievements (a great spelling test) and valiant attempts. It's the place everyone can be sure to find emergency numbers and numbers of friends to call on. You can include a family suggestion box for your intrafamily mail.

To make your bulletin board work best as "operation central" in your house:

◈ Put it somewhere where it can't be missed, such as by the front door or next to the refrigerator.
◈ When you first set it up, offer reminders to check it frequently so that everyone gets in the habit of referring to it. (Dad, when's my soccer practice? Let's look it up.)
◈ Keep pencils and plenty of paper nearby.
◈ Update it at least once a week.

48 ❧ TV Turn-Offs & Some Alternatives

There's overwhelming evidence that too much TV watching can be mind-numbing and violence-producing. Watching TV alone can frighten kids as well as giving them a skewed view of life. At the very least, indiscriminate viewing takes time away from more creative, more interactive pursuits. What are some 30-minute, mind-engaging activities to substitute for a sitcom?

◈ Choose a common item—such as a paperclip—and take turns thinking of the many ways it could be used. (For instance: to make a chain, to pry a penny out of a slot, to turn a screw, to scratch a design in a stone, to poke a hole in a piece of paper, to decorate a clay sculpture, etc., etc.)

◈ Write new words to an old song.

◈ Give everyone a story starter ("It was a dark and stormy night....") and see how many different outcomes are produced.

◈ Learn and demonstrate some magic and/or card tricks.

◈ Create collages out of old magazines.

◈ Build a model.

49 ❖ TV Turn-Ons

O kay, now that we know how bad TV can be, consider all the good that can come forth from that magic little box. TV can take us places farther than we could otherwise travel, give us glimpses of life beyond our own horizons, and provide the entry into conversation. Try these TV turn-ons:

◈ Watch together. Shared viewing of sitcoms and thrillers give you a terrific opportunity to laugh together and to question some of the action: Ask your kids if they think their favorite character in a sitcom handled a situation well or if the protagonist in a cop show could have avoided violence.

◈ Apply TV to real life. The news is frightening, even to adults. When kids view stories that they know to be true, you can reassure them that certain disasters are taking place far away and that victims are being helped. You can discuss what you might do in a similar situation. More importantly, you can help them practice empathy for victims and even give them a chance to respond practically to the needs of others. Let them see you send a donation to the Red Cross after watching a report of an earthquake, for instance.

◈ Get critical. Teach kids to question whether or not a product delivers what its commercial promises. Encourage them to look for holes in a plot and less-than-stellar acting or scripting.

◈ Plan your viewing. Use a television guide to avoid missing something worth watching.

50 ◈◈ The Bear Facts

Stuffed bears are not just for babies. And a visit to a toy store will reveal that bears—just like kids and parents—each have their own individual personalities. For a great number of reasons, including hugging and sharing secrets, everyone needs his or her own bear.

Choose each bear carefully so that its size, shape, and features reflect something about its owner. Add some individual touches, too: a striped tie on Dad's bear; a briefcase in Mom Bear's paw; ballet shoes on your aspiring dancer's bear; a mini-football helmet and team jersey on the athlete among you.

BEARIATIONS

◈ Bake cakes in bear-shaped molds and decorate accordingly.
◈ Make bears out of cut-up felt, with each adult and child gluing on personalized paraphernalia.
◈ If bears just don't do it for your clan, try Trolls, Cabbage Patch dolls, paper-bag puppets, or stuffed dinosaurs or other critters.

Part Three ⟨⟨

CONNECTING WITH
YOUR COMMUNITY

There is, within most of us, a nostalgia for a time gone by and even for a place imagined—where neighbors are neighborly, where children are free to wander, and where dogs never bark late at night. Reality, of course, intrudes, and we keep to ourselves and stay vigilant in watching over our kids. That time and place we long for probably cannot be brought back to life entirely, largely because it never really existed outside our dreams.

Living in the world has always involved a give-and-take with those around us. And the more we choose to be an active part of our communities, the greater our resources and sphere of influence become. This involvement allows us to be more satisfied with our place in the world.

51 ❧ Your Family Foundation

No doubt, you receive hundreds of appeals annually from worthy causes. Like 95% of Americans, you probably toss this "junk mail" upon its arrival. There's another option that can serve not only those seeking your help, but you and your family, too. That's setting up a charitable organization of your own, with you and your kids serving as the board of directors. Here's how it can work (feel free to change the rules however you see fit; after all, you are the benevolent boss of this enterprise):

Throughout the year, encourage your kids to put aside loose change for your charity. Set an example yourself, too. Then as the requests come in, collect them in a single box. Once a year or so convene a meeting with the other members of the board—your family—to determine which appeals appeal to you.

HOW TO CHECK OUT A CHARITY

❖ Choose a local charity that you can check on yourself. You might even choose to make a purchased donation—a classroom computer or software—for a neighborhood school or after-school program.

❖ Check with the authorities if a charity's name includes a familiar reference. For example, something called the "Police Department Children's Fund" sounds appealing. Check with your police department to confirm their involvement.

❖ Get a copy of the *Giver's Charity Rating Guide* to check out the spending patterns of 300 charitable organizations. (From the American Institute of Philanthropy, 4579 Laclede Ave., Suite 136, St. Louis, MO 63108-2103 for $3.)

52 ❧ Adopt a Neighbor

Most people don't have to look far to find someone who could use a little company or an extra hand: older people whose families have moved away, young parents who may be a bit overwhelmed at the moment, people who are caring for disabled relatives.

Without offending anyone's pride, it's possible to lend a hand or just an ear for a little while each week. You can invite this person to dinner, bring over a home-cooked meal, offer to babysit for an hour or two, bring him or her some current magazines, sweep the porch, shovel the driveway after a snowstorm.

There's no end to the need—or to the impact a small gesture of kindness can make on another human being. And just think of what your example means to your kids.

53 ❖ Volunteer at Your Child's School

Busy parents are not always in a position to drop something else in order to work at the fourth grade's bake sale. The good news is that much of the volunteer work needed by your child's school can be done at your convenience. The even better news is that your involvement with your child's school is a proven aid to your child's performance there.

BEST BETS FOR SCHOOL HELPERS

❖ Find out first just what kind of help your school needs most. Ask the principal, teacher, and other parents.

❖ Read everything that comes home with your kid—announcements of class trips, upcoming events, etc. You may be surprised that some of these events dovetail nicely with openings in your schedule. At the very least, by reading all bulletins you'll make sure that your child is prepared for any out of the ordinary school days.

❖ Consider ways in which your place of business can help out: donating used equipment (a tax deduction for your employer); providing employees with time off for tutoring local students, etc.

❖ At least once a year, try to offer your on-site services. It sends a strong message to your kid about how important school is to you.

54 ◈◈ Pot-Luck with Other Families

A nightly dinner—just the family—is a delight. An occasional night teamed up with another family can be superb. Especially if yours is a small family, the added spice brought to the table by conversations with others can help create a particularly tasty social stew.

Unlike a formal dinner at which you play host, the informality of a pot-luck dinner sets a different tone for the evening. Paper plates are okay. Odd combinations of fare add interest. Kids can sit at their own table while grown-ups savor adult conversation. Pot-lucks can be planned ahead or pulled together at a moment's notice.

Besides the pleasure of sharing a meal, pot-lucks provide a homey connection to others in the neighborhood.

55 ❖ Walk

Along with the speed and comfort of riding in a car comes a degree of isolation. Weeks can go by without seeing a neighbor who lives only a few blocks away. You may drive by a new neighborhood business a few dozen times, meaning to stop in, but never getting around to it. You may not even know about new construction, sold homes, or the addition to the local library.

Walking can put you in touch with your surroundings as no other means of transportation can. Walking is particularly good for kids to help them get a real sense for the lay of the land. Seeing a neighbor's garden up close, having a chance to chat with those you've seen but never really met, stopping at the bakery for a slow cup of coffee—these are just some of the benefits that strolling provide.

Conversations with your fellow walkers can go further when you're not having to pay as much attention to traffic and can instead focus on each other.

Another, and perhaps best, bonus is that walking naturally encourages hand-holding, something that just doesn't happen in a car.

56 ⬧⬧ Support Your Local Culture

There's more going on in your neighborhood than might first be apparent. Check local libraries, store bulletin boards, newspapers, and flyers for getting the low-down on some high brow events, where you can mingle with other like-minded patrons of the arts. Events to be on the lookout for:

- school plays
- dance and music school recitals
- art exhibits
- talks by experts in various fields of endeavor
- fund-raisers
- flea markets and garage sales
- sports exhibitions
- tours of local landmarks
- book readings and signings by authors

57 ❖ Get a Behind-the-Scenes Look at a Familiar Landmark

Whether you live in a big city or small town, there's bound to be a business or government building that houses some interesting activities that you and your family can learn more about. To visit any landmarks that are not a regular part of the normal tourist trade, you don't always need to have a class of kids or a scout troop in tow. Many will welcome just you and yours as long as you call ahead to make an appointment for your family field trip. Places that are worth exploring include:

- firehouses
- pizza shops (where you might get a chance to make your own pie)
- printing shops
- newsrooms of the local TV or newspaper
- factories (where you can learn how anything from bagels to sneakers are made)
- church choir lofts
- animal hospitals
- the local waterworks (read *The Magic Schoolbus* by Joanna Cole first)
- a photographer's studio

58 ❖ Set Up a Lemonade Stand

A kid, a sign for 5¢ lemonade, and a clear-blue sky. The image evokes a time past when a child's entrepreneurial spirit was all it took to comfort a weary summer-time traveler. So what if there's little pedestrian traffic today and the cost of ingredients alone pretty much makes this an unprofitable venture. There's still much to be gained by giving your kids a taste for operating their own roadside business. For instance, they'll practice math skills by figuring out the cost of materials (including paper cups), the price to charge, and making change. They'll learn about customer service. Wisely, you'll want to be there to supervise the activity.

Consider getting the okay to set up your stand outside a shop or after services at a nearby religious institution. Even if the kids don't make a profit, they'll gain the satisfaction of making a lot of folks smile.

RECIPE FOR LEMONADE

7 cups of water
12 tbl. of lemon juice
1-1/2 cups of sugar
1 cup of ice
1 tsp. of salt

Mix well. Serve in 6 oz. cups. Makes 1 quart (about 10 cups). Recipe may be multiplied as needed.

59 ❧ Form a Club (or Support Group)

Sharing activities that you and your family love, having someone to whom you can turn to discuss a problem, meeting others with whom you might have a lot in common—these are things that bring families together in mutually supportive ways. When you're new to a town or new to a situation, it makes sense to try to find others with whom to connect by checking around to find clubs and support groups that already exist in your area. But sometimes, you find that no such group is up and running. How do you get one going?

Start by talking to others in likely places: Ask school counselors to help hook you up to other parents of teens if you want to sponsor a teen-friendly club. Ask your pediatrician to put you in touch with other parents of kids with asthma if you need to learn more about managing this condition. Post notices at the local sporting goods store if you want to start a ski club. Check your library for a copy of *Encyclopedia of Associations*, which can provide you with names and addresses of national organizations that can offer literature and more to aid your cause or support your interests.

60 ♲ Decorate Your Home for the Season

Decorating the inside of your house for a holiday creates special memories for you and your family. Decorating the outside announces a warm welcome to passers-by. Your messages need not be elaborate; simple door wreaths, changed each season, are a friendly gesture. Other ideas worth trying out:

Spring: Flowers—in windowboxes, in pots on the porch, arranged as garlands around a window, placed bouquet-style in the hand of a garden statue.

Summer: Beach balls strung across a porch, lantern-fashion; Old Glory hung on Memorial Day (May 31), Flag Day (June 14), Independence Day (July 4), and Labor Day (1st Monday in September).

Autumn: A scarecrow sitting on a lawn chair; carved and/or painted pumpkins; harvest corn on the front door.

Winter: A fake snowman made of autumn's leaves stuffed into large white garbage bags; electric candles in the window; a bright colored bow tied to the porch light.

61 ⬥⬥ Say Thanks, Part 2

We know that thanking those nearest and dearest to us changes the way we all relate to one another. Thanking those who are just passing through our lives or who are part of it in a sort of sidelined way can make a difference, too.

Leave a note in the mailbox, just thanking the mail carrier for doing his/her job. Bring a cup of coffee to the person who works the newsstand where you buy your paper every day. The people we encounter on our regular rounds are many: busdrivers, coffee shop waiters, co-workers.

Sharing homemade cookies (or the ones you bought from your local Girl Scout) or just saying "thank you" in words to those you depend on can make you all have a richer day.

62 ❧ Write to Your Congressperson

You've got opinions about the way the world is being run. Now that you've told them to your spouse, children, and friends, where is there to go? Right to the source!

The Honorable (Name of President)
The White House
1600 Pennsylvania Avenue
Washington, D.C. 20500

The Honorable (Name of Senator)
U.S. Senate
Washington, D.C. 20510

The Honorable (Name of Representative)
U.S. House of Representatives
Washington, D.C. 20515

To reach local politicians—from the governor of your state to the community school board—check your telephone directory.

BY RETURN MAIL

Maybe you'd like the Commander-in-Chief to acknowledge your special accomplishments. You can request a presidential salute for the following events: the birth or adoption of a new family member, a wedding or anniversary celebrating 50 or more years together, Scouting awards earned by Eagle Scouts and the Girl Scouts Gold Awards, and birthdays for those 80 and over. Six weeks or so before the event, write to The White House, Greetings Office, Room 39, 1600 Pennsylvania Avenue, Washington, D.C. 20500.

63 ❖❖ Donate Gently Used Items

Now that recycling is the thing to do and retro is the fashion, consider donating what you're no longer using rather than tossing it out. Old furniture can help furnish a future for someone whose life is getting restarted. Bed linens, curtains, throw rugs, and any good-condition decorating items can turn a starter apartment from a bare shell to a cozy home. Clothing in good condition can make anyone feel better.

Group homes and other social-service agencies can use outgrown toys and sporting equipment. Non-profit resale stores can sell your used items to raise needed funds. Local schools and libraries can use or resell your cartons of books, old records, tapes, CDs, and videos. Many agencies will pick up your donations and provide you with a tax receipt.

Giving things away, and helping your kids sort through their belongings to help others puts a whole new value on things.

64 ❖ Getting to Know You

When children are still in the hand-holding stage, it's easy enough to get to know their friends—and to yank them away from any sand-tossing toddler you'd prefer that they don't get to know too well. As kids grow up and choose their own friends, it can become too easy to lose track of who these other important people in their lives are. But opening your home—and heart—to their friends allows you to see just what it is about the kid with an earring in his nose that your own kid finds worthy of friendship. How can you make your kids friends feel welcome? A random sampling of kids aged 11 to 18 offer these ideas:

❖ Have some good food available.
❖ Keep a low profile. Kids can know that you're in the house but they don't really want to engage in like long conversations or anything.
❖ It's okay to make a few inquiries—where they live, how the kids know each other, etc.
❖ It's definitely okay to invite friends to stay for dinner.
❖ If they're driving you crazy with loud music or other intrusions, privately talk to your son or daughter instead of embarrassing him or her in front of the guests.
❖ Don't engage in teenage behavior yourself. According to one poll subject, "There's nothing sadder than seeing my mom trying to act like she's sixteen again."
❖ Remember what it's like to be sixteen again.

65 ❦ Here, Kitty, Kitty

Julio has destroyed one sofa, a chair, a carpet, and countless socks. This all-black cat, with a meow that could frighten a ghost, has also awakened me during a fire, alerted me to the presence of mice, and adjusted rather well to being replaced by a child of my own species. To my kid, he offers a chance to be empathetic ("Don't yell at him, Mom, he's just a cat"), to be responsible (she freshens his water bowl daily), and to remind *me* to be more responsible ("Mom, the cat box *stinks*!").

I'd often heard that having pets prepares a person for parenthood. That, of course, is ridiculous since things like changing the litter box need be done only twice a week or so and I never have worried about Julio's grades or ability to make friends. Nevertheless, I have found that pets add a special dimension to all our lives. They remind us of our essential needs: food, shelter, love. They forgive us without reminding us of past sins. They listen. And they can be very funny.

If having a pet is at all possible, consider doing it. If your home and/or budget don't allow for adding to your family just now, find (and help your children find) ways to care for animals outside your home. Local zoos and SPCAs can help you find out about an adopt-an-animal program that allows you to contribute to the care of a species, such as a bald eagle. Or try volunteering at an animal shelter, or simply making a bird feeder with treats for the neighborhood birds.

66 ✧ Practice Random Acts of Kindness

The randomness of life often leaves us all feeling like we may have lost our footing. When disaster or just plain inconvenience strikes, we're left asking, "Why me?" The only counter, of course, is "why not?" Rather than just falling victim to the cosmos and bemoaning the failing state of humanity, we can strike back with random acts of our own making.

Unlike incorporating other trendy expressions into our vernacular, practicing random acts of kindness can have a real impact on ourselves and our communities. The opportunities are as great as everyone's need for renewed faith in humankind:

- ◈ Pay the toll of the driver behind you.
- ◈ Offer to help carry someone else's groceries.
- ◈ Pass along the magazine you've read to a fellow commuter.
- ◈ Offer your seat on the train or bus to someone else.
- ◈ Let someone in a greater hurry ahead of you on line.
- ◈ Deliver all the ingredients for a fine meal to someone who may be tiring of more affordable fare.

67 ❖ Tend a Tree

Many municipalities are a season behind in basic maintenance, let alone attempts at beautification. But in many communities, neighbors—alone or working as part of civic groups—keep decay at bay by taking over a single job.

On the Upper West Side of Manhattan, for instance, tenants on many side streets have planted flowers at the base of trees and erected small fences and polite signs that direct dogs elsewhere. The results are astounding.

In cities and towns all over, groups and individuals have turned vacant lots into community gardens, planted flowers where weeds once grew, cleared beaches and hiking trails of debris, and fostered pride in their surroundings.

Since it's a better world we're all after, remember the saying: "Think globally, but act locally."

68 ❦ Organize a Neighborhood Talent Show

Behind the brick and stucco walls of your neighbors' homes—not to mention your own home—lurks talent just waiting to be unleashed. Take a dip into the local talent pool and find out what stars of tomorrow share the sidewalk with you today.

Begin planning by scouting out a location for the performance and by booking a date at least a few weeks ahead of time, giving everyone a chance to polish-up his or her act. You can get free space by approaching certain civic centers (perhaps the library) and by planning your event during regular business hours. Or if you've got a large enough lawn or basement, host the event yourself.

Then begin to advertise for talented performers—singers, dancers, musicians, magicians, yodelers, comedians, baton twirlers, poets, actors, etc. Give everyone a time frame for his or her performances; three minutes is usually about right. Choose a Master/Mistress of Ceremonies to keep things moving. Hold at least one dress rehearsal. Advertise for an audience, too. You may wish to use the talent show as a fund-raiser for a local charity and charge admission. For neighborhood events, consider giving all performers a prize—however, you may find that this is not necessary because it's enough of a thrill to get a chance to strut one's stuff.

69 ❖ Shop Mom-and-Pop

Once upon a time (in 1955 to be exact), a guy named Ray Kroc opened a hamburger stand in downtown San Berdino, California. The neighbors came, lots of them. The rest is golden-arched history.

While most national chains did indeed begin as simple mom-and-pop operations, most mom-and-pop outlets are not destined to earn a place on the stock exchange. The proprietors of today's family businesses are competing as never before with well-established chains that can offer predictability and lower prices. There's nothing entirely wrong with that. But communities also need business owners doing business in their own neighborhoods, investing in us as much as we do in them.

Shopping in the local deli or eating at the neighborhood cafe gives us a taste for the unique and allows us to enjoy the company of the owner of the business.

70 ◈◈ Attend Services and/or Events in Another's Religious Community

Most of us go past churches, synagogues and/or mosques every day, sometimes admiring the architecture from outside but rarely venturing inside. Perhaps we're afraid we'd be seen as intruders into another's sacred space. Maybe it has simply never occurred to us to enter a religious institution that is not our own.

Before just dropping in, ask the minister or a member of the congregation for some tips on the best times to visit and any protocol that is appropriate. Some may welcome your visit only when services are not being held; others will allow you to join in at any time. Be sure to heed any advice about appropriate dress and behavior.

Helping your children learn to respect others' beliefs and rituals is as much a gift as passing on your own beliefs.

71 ◈ Make a Map of Your Neighborhood

It's a family project that can have benefits for everyone.

By mapping out their environs, young children can learn the basics of getting from here to there. Older kids can write in their friends' names, phone numbers, and addresses for quick reference; this will also help you to know where to pick them up when they're visiting their friends. If you fill in neighbors' numbers, you and your babysitters will have an easier time calling for help if you need it.

Let kids decorate your handmade neighborhood map and put it in a highly visible place.

72 ◈◈ Organize a Parade

Or a picnic. These are great ways to meet your children's friends' parents and others in the neighborhood.

One busy mother who relied on a babysitter to pick her kids up from school sent a notice (with enough copies for everyone in the class) to her daughters' teachers, suggesting a Saturday afternoon picnic in a local playground for all families in their classes. Sixty-five people showed up and she and her husband were able to get to know other parents in similar, hurried circumstances who were also anxious to get in touch with other school families.

Another mom, disappointed that her town no longer held a Fourth of July parade, organized a bicycle brigade, led by kids on tricycles, around the playground. It's become an annual tradition, complete with a marching band.

73 ◈◈ Invite a Foreign Student Home

Separated from their own families by miles and culture, college students are often left feeling pretty lonely when campuses nearly empty out during holiday breaks. Having a foreign student share your family's company and home is a gift for all concerned. Check with the student-life center at your local college for advice on how to meet a compatible student.

If possible, serve a dish that is reminiscent of his or her home along with your usual fare. Or ask the student to bring along the ingredients and to help you prepare it.

HOW TO SAY "WELCOME"
IN OTHER LANGUAGES

Language	"Welcome"
French	Bienvenue
German	Willkommen
Italian	Bevenuti
Norwegian	Velkommen
Portuguese	Boa Acolhida
Spanish	Bienvenidos
Swedish	Välkommen

74 ❧ Become Pen Pals with Another Family

To Whom It May Concern:
Some really funny things have been happening since we started this pen-pal thing. The kids have become a bit more literate, I no longer have to beg them to bring in the mail, we stop the mad rush for a few minutes about once a month to record what we've been up to. We've remembered to ask how things are going with someone else. We've learned a lot about people we'd never have met otherwise. By the way, did you know that it's summer in Australia right now as we're bundled up? My kids thought that was really neat. They especially liked learning that the water there goes down the drain counter-clockwise, instead of clockwise like it does here in the Northern Hemisphere. Now we're trying to get pen pals in Japan as well as Australia. Well, we've got to sign off now. Take care.

HOW TO GET A PEN PAL

◆ Your local children's librarian can help you locate national and international pen-pal organizations.
◆ Clubs, such as scouts, can help members in different locales find each other.
◆ Magazines often serve as meeting points, if you and/or your kids write in and request a mail meeting with others with similar concerns, hobbies, or interests.
◆ On-line computer services' bulletin boards allow network conversations. A word of caution: Supervise any correspondence your child might strike up with computer pals.

75 ❖ Take the Kids to Work

So much of our time is spent at the office or other place of business, yet our kids have very little real understanding of what we do all day. Likewise, the people we commune with daily over coffee and paperwork know little about our real lives. Introducing the kids to co-workers can bridge the gap between these two separate but intertwined parts of your life. Some pointers to make the day go smoothly:

❖ Pick a day (or an hour of the day) when the kids' presence won't intrude too much on business. Holiday times, which tend to be more relaxed, are often good choices. Or consider bringing them in on one of your days off.

❖ Dress the kids up a bit, if only to instill in them the idea that a certain degree of decorum is expected. Practice handshaking and other polite behaviors beforehand.

❖ Make sure they get to see some of your reminders of them in your workspace—their photos on your desk, their artwork on the walls, etc.

❖ While you want to show them any fun aspects of your workplace—the cafeteria, the art department, or whatever—don't be afraid to show your child that your job has its hard work and dull sides, too. Young kids, especially, will have trouble understanding why you go off without them every day to have fun. Let them know that what you do is important to the company, and to you.

Part Four ◈

Making Lemonade—
Turning Stress Points
To Your Advantage

Making the most of what life hands us is one of those lessons our mothers tried to teach us. Still, it goes against the grain to accept and even cherish the everyday stresses that are our lot without first putting up a good fight.

Here's the story of one who fought back and found, to her amazement, that life wasn't so bad after all. It's been told in many versions, but a favorite one goes something like this:

A woman, tired of living with her noisy and demanding family, went to the rabbi to ask his advice. "Tonight, bring the chickens from the coop inside, and things will be better," he said. She did

that, but things got worse. She returned to the rabbi, who advised her to bring the cows in from the barn. This was done, but nothing improved. Over the course of a week, she went back for more advice. Each evening, the rabbi suggested that she bring one more beast into her home. The noise became unbearable. In desperation, she returned to the rabbi, pleading for a means to find some peace and quiet. "Tonight, remove the goats," he said. Over the course of a week, he advised her to remove the other animals, including the cows, and, finally, the chickens.

At last, with only her family at home, things seemed very peaceful, indeed.

76 ◈ A Do-Nothing Day

By nature, families are messy. Not necessarily unkempt or sloppy, but emotionally messy. Anger and love spill over into one another, making a familial stew that doesn't always taste quite right. You and your family put demands on one another because you have to. But, let's face it: It's not always easy to respond to the needs of others with a smile. Wouldn't it be nice if once in a while you all were freed from rules of the house?

One writer in *Sesame Street Parents' Guide*, described her family's "Templeton Holidays," named for the slovenly rat in *Charlotte's Web*. On such days, the rules for civilized behavior were more-or-less suspended. Even toothbrushing was optional. No one developed any seriously bad habits in this 24-hour free-for-all, she noted. In fact, they all replenished some of their humor and found time to get reacquainted.

SOME THINGS YOU AND YOUR FAMILY CAN DO INSTEAD OF FOLLOWING RULES

◈ Play Chinese Checkers. If you forget how to play, make it up as you go along.
◈ Rent tapes and make a few batches of popcorn for dinner.
◈ Let your children teach you the words to a current song.
◈ Draw, paint, or do a jigsaw puzzle together.
◈ Go someplace where you can walk barefoot.
◈ Read aloud to each other.

77 ✧ Start a Family Business

Before deciding that you can't afford to take that longed-for family vacation or purchase a much-wanted but too expensive item, consider a short-term business venture. What kinds of businesses require little capital investment, involve the whole family, and can raise hundreds of dollars in a few months? Consider:

❖ Car washing in your driveway (charge 50¢ less per service than the commercial outfits in your neighborhood).

❖ Kiddie party-planning and clean-up service (charge by the hour, by the kid, and/or by adding a percentage to the cost of purchased items).

❖ Holiday shopping service (charge by the hour, plus a percentage of the purchase prices).

❖ Marketing a talent or skill: photography, gardening, sewing, housepainting, math tutoring, babysitting, typing (charge the going rate).

78 ❖ Practice the Art of Humor

"Knock-knock"
"Who's there?"
"Boo"
"Boo-who?"
"Don't cry!"

It's a favorite among the four- and five-year-old crowd in our house, and besides being one of the few oft-repeated jokes that has nothing to do with the bathroom, it pretty much sums up that life offers both tears and laughter. Whenever possible, opt for the laughter.

As an alternative to nagging: Instead of shouting that you're going to take away roller-blading privileges for a month if your son doesn't learn to put his skates away, try leaving a note attached to the skates that goes something like this: "Dear Jeremy, I'm really scared. Here I am on the staircase in harm's way. Someone could step on me and break a ball bearing, for Pete's sake! Mom could see me here and put me away in the garage. You know how much I hate that place. Please, put me in the hall closet where I belong. I'll be much happier there. Thanks—Your loyal skates."

As an antidote to mild blues: Kids sulk. Adults sulk. It's natural. It's human. It can get really boring. Injecting a little humor is, as they say at *Reader's Digest*, "the best medicine." Read a funny story aloud, repeat a joke you've heard, watch a classic comedy together. Let the mood lighten.

As a vocabulary builder: So many funny lines result from plays on words. A teacher, trying to make a point to her sixth-graders, said that "It's important to know your facts before writing a report" to which one kid, in all sincerity, announced that "my mom never lets me touch the fax machine." Help your young kids see and hear the funny possibilities around them all day: If there are picnic ants, where are the uncles? If someone's "off the wall," did he hurt himself falling down? Expect the kids to churn out a few yucks as they roll their eyes at you. In the meantime, though, they'll be learning to appreciate the absurd just a bit better.

79 ◈◈ Eat a Healthful Meal

There's not always time to eat (let alone cook) a well-balanced meal, but a steady diet of thawed dinners and take-out food is short on more than just nutrition. Foods prepared in a hurry are not savored. Lingering over a fulfilling meal, however, encourages conversation and makes everyone feel well-cared for.

While conflicting and overextending schedules may make preparing a feast every night impossible, a regularly scheduled "from scratch" family meal, in which everyone helps out, satisfies both body and soul. Some "ingredients" to include in your planning:

Time: Plan for a night when no one's in a hurry—no homework to do, no meetings to attend later on, no need to get to bed particularly early.

Quiet: Tune out TV, radio, and family debates.

Appeal: Be sure that the menu includes something that each family member really likes, even if that means serving mashed potatoes as well as French fries.

Touch of Class: Light candles, use the good china, serve milk from a pitcher, etc.

Surprise: Prepare a small surprise to be served with (or as) dessert: fortune cookies with personalized fortunes; tickets for a family outing; the tape of a movie you've all been wanting to see.

80 ❖ Initiate Soothing Rituals

O ur hectic schedules—if we ever bothered to write down the thousand-and-one things we do every day—would exhaust Atlas. Maybe it's time for a back rub. In the course of the daily grind, there are opportunities for soothing moments that take no added time, but that add immeasurably to our sense of belonging and of being nurtured. When bathing or dressing younger children, take a moment to massage their little hands and feet. Don't intrude on older kids' space but instead institute an at-least-once-a-day hug. Find the way that works best for your family to say goodnight and make it a habit. Carry on cultural and religious rituals, such as candle lighting, with the kids playing as much of a role as they're able.

81 ❖❖ Designate "Family Time"

Imagine an hour, a morning, or a whole day each week that allowed for no outside intrusion, no other places to be. At first, it may be difficult to splice off a bit of time to do nothing but enjoy one another's company. But it's worth the effort. While your family will find its own unique way of coming together, these ideas may help get you started:

❖ Let each family member take turns choosing how to spend this week's family time.
❖ Have a few ground rules: everyone must be included; no excuses for opting out; interruptions (such as telephone calls) are for emergencies only.
❖ Mark the time on the family calendar to help steer you around it as you make other plans.

82 ◈ Attach Rewards to Tasks Completed

Getting the laundry done buys you a half-hour for drinking a cup of tea. Tax preparation earns you a much bigger reward—an evening out. Homework done before Sunday night gets your eight-year-old an hour of Monopoly with you. The lists of tasks for each of us is long, but so is the list of little pleasures that we'd enjoy. Linking the work to the reward is not really bribery; think of it as more of an incentive program. It's a great self-motivator and does wonders for encouraging kids to get with the program. And besides, wouldn't *you* rather hear "If you clean your room, we'll have time to go out for pizza," than "No pizza for you if that room isn't straightened up!"

SPECIAL REWARDS COUPONS

Formalize your bargaining by creating coupon books that indicate which reward follows which activity. Allow kids to pick a few each week to redeem as earned. Here's a sample:

```
IF YOU: WASH THE CAR
YOU EARN: A MOVIE
```

83 ❖ Play Hooky with Your Kids

Sure, it's important to be responsible and to raise our kids with a sense of playing by the rules. But every once in a while, we all need a break from responsibility. For some families, conspiring together to take time off midweek works best. Others find it most fun to break formation spontaneously. Done infrequently, this minor slacking off can result in renewed energy for weeks to come. From parents and kids who've taken these unauthorized breaks, come these recollections:

❖ *Mom woke me up and whispered in my ear, "Instead of you going to school and me going to work, how about going to the beach?" I couldn't believe it. It was like winning the lottery or something. The beach was real empty and it was great.*—Megan, age 9

❖ *We were having a rotten morning, running late, screaming at each other. It was the third day out of three that we were just not functioning right. Everything was just too rushed. Without thinking much about it, I called in sick, called both my kids' schools, and made plans to take them to a movie we all wanted to see. No one died from missing a day doing what we were supposed to be doing. After the movie, we made a deal to be nicer to one another in the mornings and we've pretty much stuck to it.*—a mom

❖ *In our family, we play hooky together twice a year—on the first day of winter, which gives us a nice pre-holiday break, and on the first day of spring. It's a tradition that my wife's mother began with her family and that we really like keeping up.*—a dad

84 ◈◈ Cuddle Up Together

When my daughter was born, my sister-in-law sent me a plaque that reads in part: "So quiet down cobwebs/Dust, go to sleep/I'm rocking my baby/And babies don't keep."

With a job that kept me on the run more hours than I could count, I'd long ago learned to ignore dust. But learning to put aside all the "important" things to take time to cuddle was a message worth displaying in those first months of exhausted motherhood. This little reminder still helps as the hours and days gather into years.

Preschoolers insist on a minimum number of hugs a day. As the kids get older and a public kiss can result in a could-kill look, cuddling becomes a bit more of a challenge. But everyone, no matter what age, needs loving, physical touch. One mother found that her son would accept a quick "hand-hug," a short, tight squeeze in lieu of a full-blown bear hug after school. At age ten, he is even willing to initiate such shows of affection. Another family has made a bedtime ritual of piling into Mom and Dad's bed for fifteen minutes or so for chatting and hugging each night.

85 ❧ Let Kids Practice Making Decisions

Much of life is based on habits, and some of us have developed one of two habitual responses to any kid-generated demand: Either we take a "because-I-said-so" stance and try to get our kids to do things our way, or we work feverishly to fulfill their every whim. Both ways leave parents exhausted and kids a bit lost. What works in many families is for parents (who have the right of veto power) and kids to negotiate a system of taking turns in family decision-making, raising the stakes as the kids mature. Begin with the small stuff to give kids practice in making decisions and in living with their consequences:

- Let kids choose what they'll eat from a list of acceptable alternatives.
- Likewise, let them choose their clothing within a seasonably appropriate range.
- Let them try out a couple of places and varying time slots at which they find it most productive to do homework. Allow for trial and error.
- Include them in the decision about where they'll go to camp, where your family will vacation, and how you'll all spend your free time together.
- Give guidance, but allow them some control over their finances. Telling them that a particular toy is a waste of money won't be as effective as learning about value themselves.
- Try not to judge their friends by appearances only.
- Talk about the process of decision-making—yours as well as theirs.

86 ❧ Apologize

One of the silliest lines ever said in a feature film came from *Love Story*, the 1970s hit, which immortalized the phrase, "Love means never having to say you're sorry." There are few people who would actually want to share a life with someone who held that concept near and dear.

In real life, we all screw up sometimes. Saying "I'm sorry" lets those we love know that it's us, not them, who blew it. In a typical scenario, a bad day at the office spills over into family time and we meet a kid's normal misbehavior or demand for attention with an explosion. It's understandable. It happens to just about everyone at one time or another. A show of anger, even misplaced anger, is not fatal. But it can hurt and confuse kids just the same.

When we stop to say, "You really didn't deserve that" and explain some of what's really got you upset, you accomplish three important things:

1. You tend to your child's hurt and restore his or her sense of safety
2. You teach them that anger need not escalate
3. You teach them by your own example about taking responsibility for one's actions.

The next time *they* make a mistake, they'll have a road map showing how to back up and try again.

87 ✦ Do Homework Together

You've got bills to pay and office work to finish up after dinner. The kids, of course, have their book reports and spelling reviews. You can each go off to your own corners of the house to accomplish your work with as little distraction as possible. Or you can use this time to be together quietly.

One night I was getting so annoyed by Jillian's constant calling out to me for answers to questions about her homework. It was things like, "Mom, how do you spell Hawaii?" and "Where's the calculator?" I was trying to do our taxes and her interruptions were making me crazy. But then it occurred to me that we'd only had a few hours together that whole week and what Jillian really wanted was my company. Her questions were just an excuse to make contact. So I moved us both to the dining room table. After a few minutes there, she stopped checking in with me and kept to her work. I got mine done, too. Now we make it a habit to work together. It's less lonely for each of us.

—JoHanna

88 ❖ Surrender

We spend a lot of time and energy trying to keep our worlds on schedule, in order, and running smoothly. Then one day, you or your child wake up with the flu or the babysitter calls up to say she won't be able to make it or the dishwasher overflows as you're heading out the door. The usual response to a crisis for most responsible adults is to jump right in and try to make everything right, to do whatever needs doing to get back on track as soon as possible.

Sometimes, though, it's a good idea to cancel the day instead. The world won't fall apart if you decide to slow down, stay home and take care of yourself, or have an unscheduled interruption for one day. To surrender to circumstances allows us to put things in perspective. It gives us practice in letting go of our need to be in control. It reminds us to live in the present. And it gives everyone who depends on us a taste of self-sufficiency.

89 ❧ Meet Your Kids for School Lunch

Y ou know how boring it can get to eat the same lunch in the same place, often right at your desk, every day. Chances are good that your kids could use a little change of venue and a switched menu, too.

Younger kids will love it when you surprise them at lunch by taking them out of the cafeteria and into the nearest fast-food place. Older kids may prefer a bit of warning, since their social lives will be affected.

In any case, check with your child's school to make arrangements for your private lunch beforehand.

90 ❖ The $5 Solution

True, the best things in life are free. But once in a while, some cold cash can do wonders for binding your family together. The next time your kids are bickering or whenever you see some evidence that you're all not being as thoughtful to one another as you'd all like, call a family meeting. Give each member $5 (or whatever amount that you can afford and that seems like quite a bit of cash to your kids) with the instruction that each person is to spend it on the person seated to his or her right.

Additional ground rules:

❖ No one can ask the person who's buying his or her gift for anything specific.
❖ Each person is to spend one day really thinking about what his or her recipient would like.
❖ No gifts for oneself in the guise of a gift for a sibling, child, or parent.

91 ◈ Get the Lowdown on Kids' Days

How was your day?" "Okay." "What did you do?" "Nothing."
Figuring that the kids are in school about 180 days a year and perhaps at camp or another summer program for another 40, you can almost bet that you'll have the above conversation about 37,180 times in the course of their school years.

Maybe its something in the school lunches that makes kids lose all memory before they reach home ready to share the details with you. Without prying too much, you can get in on the events of your child's day in a few ways:

◈ Volunteer details about your own work day, rather than painting in broad strokes. Instead of saying, "Boy! Was work ever hectic today," offer that "I talked to 102 customers today. That's a record."
◈ Be specific with your questions, too. A "How was lunch?" will get you an "Okay." But a "Did they serve those awful fish sticks again?" might get you a "No, today it was gross hot dogs in some kind of sauce." Such details will help you know what *not* to serve for dinner tonight.
◈ Go for the superlatives: "What was the most ridiculous thing you saw today?" "What was the best part of your day?" "What was the worst?"
◈ Check the backpacks of younger kids.

92 ❧ Bring Home a Souvenir of Your Day

Well, Mom and Dad, what did *you* do all day? Kids are curious about adult time-away-from-home, too, though they're a bit too self-centered to think to ask you about it.

Bridge the gap by bringing home souvenirs of your day: a few mints from the restaurant where you ate lunch, a silly doodling you did while on the phone, the squishy packing material that accompanied your new computer (which can also be used for art projects).

Raise the stakes when traveling on business, bringing back a mug or t-shirt from the city you visited. The actual item doesn't matter. But your children will relish the reminder that you think of them even when you can't be with them.

93 ❧ Home-Alone Touchpoints

You've reviewed safety procedures enough for both you and your child to feel prepared for an emergency. You've discussed the ground rules about TV, having friends over, and going outside. But it's still not easy to relax at work knowing that your young teen is home alone after school. Admit it or not, he or she may be feeling a bit anxious too. What are some of the things you can do to make sure that during your child's home-alone time you're still in touch?

◈ Have at least one set time for calling in. If you'll be away from your desk, leave a number where you can be reached or a message about when you'll return.
◈ Insist that your child let you know where he or she will be if not at home.
◈ Have two copies of a list of neighbors' names and telephone numbers available—one posted at home and one with you—whom either of you can call on when necessary.
◈ Occasionally, leave little notes to your kid in places he or she is sure to look, such as the refrigerator, saying, "Hi, I can't wait to come home and hug you."
◈ Limit the time your child is alone by helping him or her find fun, afterschool activities in which to participate. Five solo afternoons a week is too much for most kids.
◈ Though kids need some downtime and shouldn't be given adult responsibilities, once in a while, ask them to complete a chore or even get dinner ready. Let the payoff be more time with you later in the evening.

94 ⬥⬥ Exercise Together

When you hear the word *lap*, what comes to mind?
a) the distance from one end of a swimming pool to the other, or
b) the seat formed when you sit down

If you answered "a," consider inviting your kids to join you for your workout. Matt, a stockbroker and father of a five-year-old son, finds that the best way to unwind from his tense days is to take a mile run through his local park, an activity that was taking away even more time from his son. So he asked Graham to join him, changing his pace to accommodate shorter legs. Now instead of another half-hour away from one another, they spend an hour running, walking, and talking.

If you answered "b," jogging your memory to recall the last time you voluntarily worked up a sweat may be all the workout you can take right now. But making time for getting physical strengthens more than your cardiovascular system. Find an activity that you can start slowly and do at varying levels of competence. Visit local gyms for information about family programs. If working out indoors and in private is more your style, check out the video store for fun-to-follow exercise tapes, including ones designed specifically for kids.

95 ❖❖ While You're Away...

Business, both personal and corporate, sometimes takes us away from our families for days at a time. You can ease the pain of separation by checking in often and by planning ahead:

- For young children who can't quite grasp the meaning of "six days," mark a calendar to show how long it will be from now until then.
- Tape record yourself reading a favorite bedtime story.
- Leave notes, one to be opened each night or each morning.
- Send a postcard in a first-class mail envelope to arrive home before you do. (First-class envelopes arrive in about two days, while postcards can take a week or more.)
- Have kids create a daily log of what they'll want to tell you upon your return.
- Call home at a set time each day.

96 ❖ Make Your Own Holiday Cards

The average year provides few opportunities for correspondence with family and friends. While getting the holiday cards out can seem to be just one more thing on the "to-do" list, enlisting the kids' creativity can turn a chore into a worthy rainy-day activity. The trick is to have the raw materials available to serve up at the right time. Some ideas:

❖ Save last year's cards and hand them out on an otherwise boring day. Have the kids cut out the pictures on the front to glue onto folded construction paper.
❖ If your kids are proficient on a computer, ask them to design and print out your cards.
❖ Make fingerpaint handprints on folded construction paper.
❖ Cut out designs—stars, trees, etc.—on kitchen sponges and let kids spongepaint with fingerpaints on blank paper.
❖ Copy a favorite photo or use a batch of photos to paste onto the front of folded paper.
❖ Handprint or type your inside message, photocopy enough copies, and have kids paste these inside each card.

97 ⊛ Turn Over Some Playful Work to the Kids

Chances are good that you have too much to do. Chances are also good that your kids sometimes complain of having nothing to do. There's a solution here. Turn over some of the more pleasant but still time-consuming tasks to them.

A hint for assuring their cooperation: Do as Tom Sawyer did—begin the job yourself in full view of the kids and let them take the lead in asking to be allowed to help. For starters, suggest that they:

- organize and insert family photos into an album
- sort and box the holiday ornaments and other decorations
- write their own birthday party invitations
- make centerpieces for holiday and other special-occasion meals
- wrap presents
- put stamps on envelopes

98 ◈◈ Line Up Some Diversions

Waiting on line is inevitable. Being bored during your wait is not. Capture your kids' fancy and save your own sanity by carrying a few diversions along on your outings.

Some can be of the tangible variety—playing cards, joke and story books, hand-held games. Others require only your imagination. Play word games, for example. How many things can you and your child find that begin with the letter "M"? How many square-shaped items? How many green ones?

Other observation games to try include "Who Am I?" in which each player takes a turn describing an item within the scenery as the other players try to guess what that player is describing. For instance, "I am yellow. I have a jacket. I taste good with ice cream. What am I?" (A banana.) Play mental bingo, by naming nine items for others to find around them.

99 ✎ Have a Parents' Night Out

Family togetherness has its limits. There are times when kids need to be with other kids and when parents need to leave the kids at home and have a bit of one-on-one time all their own. If you and your spouse are hesitant about leaving the kids for an evening or even a weekend, you're not alone. Many parents deny themselves each other, rationalizing that they're away from the children too much already because of work or that family togetherness means the *whole* family or that it simply costs too much to get away. Single parents especially need time alone with other adults.

Consider these counter rationalizations before you decide to stay home playing Parcheesi with the kids next Saturday night:

◈ Kids need to know in no uncertain terms that their parents like each other enough to want to be together and have fun together.
◈ Kids need to know that you and your spouse have interests beyond parenthood.
◈ Kids need to know that growing up and being a responsible parent doesn't mean giving up being a person who's capable of having fun.
◈ You can get free babysitting by trading off with other like-minded parents.
◈ Kids need the opportunity to learn to relate to another source of nurturance—whether it be from a teenaged babysitter, a friend's parents, or from grandparents.

100 ◈ Put Things in Perspective

There are in the life of every family some truly awful days, when nothing seems to be going right. Money might be tight. You or one of your kids may be having a rough time at work or school. You may be fighting among yourselves. When little things threaten to overtake us, it helps to stop and look at our lives in a greater content.

One new mother of a colicky baby learned to say, mantra-style, "Thank God she can scream," as she heaped one sleepless night upon another pacing the floor with her crying baby. Knowing that a friend's child was not strong enough for whimpering helped her see her son's colic for the transitory thing it was.

Sometimes it helps to compartmentalize our lives: When work and/or money matters are threatening to unravel us, take extra pleasure from the parts of your life that *are* doing fine. Illness and loss will undermine the strongest among us. Appreciating and acknowledging the help and care of friends can help carry us through. Anger at one another can be a catalyst for necessary change, rather than an excuse for emotional withdrawal when we stop to think of what's really at stake.

Certainly, we don't have to dismiss all our own disappointments and anxieties as trivial. As humans, we are not meant to. But sometimes stepping back gives us a chance to see our lives against a wider background and to discover that what we have in front of us isn't so bad.